# S·E·W·A·N·E·E
## Grace Revealed

# S·E·W·A·N·E·E
## Grace Revealed

A BOOK OF PHOTOGRAPHY BY
### Katharine Gamble Scrantom

*For my family:*

*Billy, Katie,*
*Margaret, and Gamble*

*Trust in the Lord with all your heart*
*    and do not rely on your own insight.*
*In all your ways acknowledge him,*
*    and he will make straight your paths.*

*...keep sound wisdom and discretion;*
*    let them not escape from your sight,*
*and they will be life for your soul and*
*    adornment for your neck.*
*Then you will walk on your way securely*
*    and your foot will not stumble.*
*                — PROVERBS 3:5-6, 21-23 RSV*

# F·O·R·E·W·O·R·D
## The Very Reverend Guy Fitch Lytle

Sewanee is a place: a physical place in the South, a small village on what we, in this part of the country, can call a mountain. It is a beautiful place, even in the bleak mid-winter of ice and snow. In the dogwood springs and verdant summers, it becomes almost Eden-like, marred only—like its prototype—by snakes and sinful humans. Even the melancholic colors of fall and the ghostly embrace of frequent fog enhance the visual wonders of the Domain.

Most days and nights (allowing for a few party weekends) convey a serene surface. People with active professions in the big cities of the South come here on weekends and in the summers to relax and restore their lives. But they also come for the intellectual, spiritual and personal stimulation of this place. Sewanee is not an isolated, sleepy Brigadoon. It is a sophisticated community, only five miles off a very busy interstate highway. It is full of tradition, but also fully aware of the changes and problems of the modern world. And that is how life should be: life, not caricature.

Sewanee is also a spiritual place, an intentional community of learning and worship. It is a place where, for more than a century, people have come or been sent, to develop their minds and their souls. A place where those set on a common and noble purpose have walked through doors of enchantment and edification, and have begun life-long friendships. A place from which people have gone forth to love and serve the Lord, to make a difference in a great variety of vocations, to better the common good.

Sewanee is, thirdly, a place in the imagination. Both for those of us who live here and those who come and leave, certain visual images stay in our minds. When we think of "Sewanee," we see the memorial cross or All Saints' Chapel, a favorite pathway or bluff view, a sleeping dog or children on a class outing from the elementary school. Sights and sounds, faces and voices make our memories.

Sewanee's special beauty and ethos have attracted many excellent photographers, and their visions have filled picture books, official publications, the *Mountain Messenger*, and many private albums. Recently for three years, Sewanee was graced by the presence of Katharine Gamble Scrantom. While her husband Billy studied for ordination, she contributed her personal faith and extraordinary eye to our ongoing task of understanding who we are. One of the finest portrait photographers I have ever known, she also took a series of descriptive and narrative shots that seem to me to capture the spirit of Sewanee in a very special way. These images are her reading of the Sewanee she experienced.

A person of deep religious faith, Kathy often thought of passages of Scripture or hymns or meditations when she saw a picture. She would ask others what they "heard" when they observed her photographs. This book contains a selection of those "images with words." I welcome this attempt to express "Sewanee" both as a physical place and as images of the heart and soul. I hope that it will evoke your own memories or anticipation of life on the Mountain and will be a source of inspiration for *your* reflection on your time in this place.

—THE VERY REV'D DR. GUY FITCH LYTLE, III
DEAN, THE SCHOOL OF THEOLOGY

# I·N·T·R·O·D·U·C·T·I·O·N

*Katharine Gamble Scrantom*

For years, photography was my art, my public expression. Christianity was my private life, known only to a select few. Several years ago, I began to realize how hard it was to keep my two passions separate, and, with God's help, I began to integrate my public and private personae. God's grace over time has united my faith and my art, and it was during my stay in Sewanee, Tennessee, that the sufficiency of God's grace was revealed.

For three years, while my husband studied at the School of Theology, I roamed, observed, and captured the special images of the Mountain. I found freedom on the Domain to focus on what God wanted me to photograph, to follow my own path to the art and faith I desired to unite in photographic expression. My Sewanee friends, mentors, and acquaintances urged me to publish my work, and offered meditations, scripture, hymns, and poetry to accompany these photographs. This book of meditations and photography is a reflection of the refreshing changes in my life.

During the second year of seminary, our family spent the summer in Pine Mountain, Georgia. There—through the unlikely messenger of our Sewanee-born part Golden Retriever, Lucky—I witnessed a personal parable I will never forget. Each morning, Lucky and I left the family home for a brisk walk around the lake. The lake was a quiet place to relax, think, and pray. We came to love this early morning routine; the trails seemed to become our very own. But we were not completely alone. As we walked on the lake road, past the first few neighboring houses, two energetic canine friends always joined us. We would leave the pavement and enter our trail, Lucky racing ahead of her two new buddies.

Our usual route took us across a small wooden bridge over a stream. The dogs always ran ahead of me across the bridge—the two visitors easily bounding across its wide-spaced wooden slats. But not Lucky. Each time Lucky crossed the bridge, her feet would slip and fall into the cracks. She stumbled, lost control, and fell with pained yelps. For two weeks she followed her friends. Each time she reached this passage, I noticed her frustration, how she whimpered and faced the bridge in fear. She wanted to follow her friends.

But this particular morning was different. As the other two dogs leaped across the wooden slats and ran into the woods, Lucky just stood there pondering the awful task before her. She didn't move a muscle, staring at the bridge. All of a sudden, with what seemed a look of discernment, she tore off to the right, went excitedly down the bank to the stream, swam across, and climbed up the other side. After a good shake, she glanced back at me with a look of confidence and ran off to catch up with the other dogs. In a minute, the four of us were together again, soaking up the wonders around us.

Thereafter, each time we walked the lake trail, Lucky took her new path across the stream, bypassing the menace of the bridge. She realized she could not be just like the others. She found her *own* new way to make it to the other side.

What a gift I had been given that morning! Later, back in Sewanee, I realized the importance of this lesson for my own life's impasse: how I could merge my photography and my faith without fear of being misunderstood. As I reflected on Lucky's epiphany, I realized each of us often tries, with frustration, to travel a path God didn't intend for us to follow. With the different gifts and talents given to us, and, with God's guidance, we are able to forge our own way forward on the unique path our Creator planned. Quite often, it takes time for us to mature and find the way—and it takes God's grace.

The book before you, I trust, is a revelation of the amazing God-breathed beauty of Sewanee. But beyond the images, I pray you will find a quiet place to meditate on the grace of God. A peaceful, purposeful, still life of spirituality is often awakened by time spent in the beauty of creation. Sewanee is such a place.

I thank God for introducing me to the art of photography. And I am grateful that at age seventeen, I first deeply understood the path to God through Jesus Christ—at a time when I most needed God's love, forgiveness, and the ability to forgive.

All my life, my parents found unique ways to support my artistry:  Thanks to my mother, Jane Leach Gamble Claiborne, for her devotion, childlike faith, and unconditional love. I passed many happy and quiet hours in the darkroom that she had built for me at sixteen. I appreciate my dad, the late Bush Louis Gamble, for his unconditional love and for my first camera (*his camera*). From observing his life, I learned to see past the surface—into those guarded places where the truest parts of each of us reside.

In college I met my husband Billy. The first time he saw a photograph of mine, he expressed its meaning better than I could ever have articulated. His unfailing support of "my addiction" includes repeatedly carrying heavy loads of equipment in from the car. This book would not be what it is without his helpful creativity and constructive insight. For Billy, I give ultimate thanks and blessings.

I am so grateful to my three wonderful children, Katie, Margaret, and Gamble, for their patience during all the times I had them wait in the B.C. darkroom for my prints to be plucked from the developing wash; for listening to me talk about the pictures and this book; for loving art, and learning so much throughout the entire birthing of this book.

Katie, Margaret, Gamble, and Billy have been, and are yet, the most loving, patient, and supportive family a person could have. This book, *Sewanee: Grace Revealed*, is dedicated to these four special children of God.

—APRIL, 1998

THE UNIVERSITY PRAYER

*Almighty God, the Father of our Lord Jesus Christ,*
*we Thy servants implore Thy blessing upon this University.*
*Give the spirit of Wisdom to all those to whom*
*Thou hast given the authority of teaching and of government.*
*Let the students grow in grace day by day;*
*enlighten their minds, purify their hearts, and sanctify their wills.*
*Bless all who have contributed to this institution;*
*and raise up to the University, we humbly pray Thee,*
*a never-failing succession of benefactors;*
*through our Lord and Savior, Jesus Christ.*

Amen.

*And your ancient ruins shall be rebuilt;*
*you shall raise up the foundations of*
*many generations;*
*you shall be called the repairer of*
*the breach;*
*the restorer of streets to dwell in.*
                        —ISAIAH 58:12 RSV

Heaven's Gate, 1995

*Although within us there are wounds,*
*Lord Christ, above all there is*
*the miracle of your mysterious presence.*
*Thus, made lighter or even set free,*
*we are going with you, the Christ,*
*from one discovery to another.*
—Brother Roger of Taizé

Untitled, 1996

*But what happiness, what security, what pleasure it is to have a friend "with whom you would dare to speak just as you would speak to yourself!" You would not fear to confide to a friend about your failings, nor would you blush to reveal to him your spiritual progress; and will you not entrust your plans for the future to the one to whom you have committed all the secrets of your heart?*

*And, in this respect, friendship excels everything I've just said, for friendship is a path that leads very close to the perfection which consists of the enjoyment and knowledge of God, such that a man who is a friend of man is made into a friend of God, according to what the Savior said in the gospel: "Now I will not call you servants, but my friends."*

—AELRED OF RIEVAULX

Untitled, 1996

*Extol the Lord our God,*
*and worship at his holy mountain;*
*for the Lord our God is holy!*
—PSALM 99:9 RSV

Even in the Fog, The Lord is Present, 1993

*Lead, kindly Light, amid the encircling gloom,*
　　*Lead thou me on:*
*The night is dark, and I am far from home;*
　　*Lead thou me on:*
*Keep thou my feet; I do not ask to see the distant scene;*
　　*one step enough for me.*

　　　　　　　　　—JOHN HENRY NEWMAN, 1833

*I will not forget you.*
*Behold, I have graven you on the palms of my hands.*

—ISAIAH 49:15-16 RSV

Mrs. Chitty, 1994

*God, give us grace to accept with serenity the things that cannot be changed, courage to change the things that should be changed, and the wisdom to distinguish the one from the other.*

—SERENITY PRAYER

Untitled, 1996

*I lift up my eyes to the hills.*
*From whence does my help come?*
*My help comes from the Lord,*
*who made heaven and earth.*

*He will not let your foot be moved,*
*he who keeps you will not slumber.*
*Behold he who keeps Israel*
*will neither slumber nor sleep.*

*The Lord is your keeper;*
*the Lord is your shade*
*on your right hand.*
*The sun shall not smite you by day,*
*nor the moon by night.*

*The Lord will keep you from all evil,*
*he will keep your life.*
*The Lord will keep your going out and your coming in*
*from this time forth*
*and for evermore.*

—PSALM 121, A SONG OF ASCENTS RSV

Subtle Embrace, 1994

*I learn, as the years roll onward*
*and leave the past behind*
*That much I had counted sorrow*
*But proves that God is kind;*
*That many a flower I had longed for*
*Had hidden a thorne of pain,*
*And many a rugged bypath*
*Led to fields of ripened grain.*

*The clouds that cover the sunshine*
*They cannot banish the sun;*
*And the earth shines out the brighter*
*When the weary rain is done.*
*We must stand in the deepest shadow*
*To see the clearest light;*
*And often through wrong's own darkness*
*Comes the very strength of light.*

*The sweetest rest is at even,*
*After a wearisome day,*
*When the heavy burden of labor*
*Has borne from our hearts away;*
*And those who have never known sorrow*
*Can not know the infinite peace*
*That falls on the troubled spirit*
*When it sees at least release.*

*We must live through the dreary winter*
*If we would value the spring;*
*And the woods must be cold and silent*
*Before the robins sing.*
*The flowers must be buried in darkness*
*Before they can bud and bloom,*
*and the sweetest, warmest sunshine*
*Comes after the storm and gloom.*

—UNKNOWN

Untitled, 1996

*Whatsoever things are true,*
*Whatsoever things are honest,*
*Whatsoever things are just,*
*Whatsoever things are pure,*
*Whatsoever things are lovely,*
*Whatsoever things are of good report,*
*If there be any virtue,*
*and if there be any praise,*
*think on these things.*
                —PHILIPPIANS 4:8 KJV

Untitled, 1996

*We glory in your cross, O Lord,*
*and praise and glorify your holy resurrection;*
*for by virtue of your cross*
*joy has come to the whole world.*
    —ANTHEM 1, BOOK OF COMMON PRAYER

Grace, 1996

*Bread of the world, in mercy broken,*
*Wine of the soul, in mercy shed,*
*by whom the words of life were spoken,*
*and in whose death our sins are dead:*
*look on the heart by sorrow broken,*
*look on the tears by sinners shed;*
*and be they feast to us the token*
*that by thy grace our souls are fed.*
          —REGINALD HEBER (1783-1826)

*All things bright and beautiful,*
*all creatures great and small,*
*all things wise and wonderful,*
*the Lord God made them all.*
—CECIL FRANCES ALEXANDER (1818-1895)

Untitled, 1996

*Surely it is God who saves me;*
*I will trust in him and not be afraid.*
*For the Lord is my stronghold and my sure defense,*
*and he will be my Savior.*
*Therefore you shall draw water with rejoicing*
*from the spring of salvation.*
*And on that day you shall say,*
*Give thanks to the Lord and call upon his Name;*
*Make his deeds known among the peoples;*
*see that they remember that his Name is exalted.*
*Sing the praises of the Lord, for he has done great things,*
*and this is known in all the world.*
*Cry aloud, inhabitants of Zion, ring out your joy,*
*for the great one in the midst of you is the Holy One of Israel.*
—THE FIRST SONG OF ISAIAH, BOOK OF COMMON PRAYER

Surely, It is God Who Saves Me, 1996

*For I am already on the point of being sacrificed; the time of my departure has come. I have fought the good fight, I have finished the race, I have kept the faith. Henceforth there is laid up for me the crown of righteousness, which the Lord, the righteous judge, will award to me on that Day, and not only to me but also to all who have loved his appearing.*

—2 TIMOTHY 4:6-8 RSV

Sewanee Gate, 1993

*We thank you, Almighty God, for the gift of water. Over it the Holy Spirit moved in the beginning of creation. Through it you led the children of Israel out of their bondage in Egypt into the land of promise. In it your Son Jesus received the baptism of John and was anointed by the Holy Spirit as the Messiah, the Christ, to lead us, through his death and resurrection, from the bondage of sin into everlasting life.*

—PRAYER AT HOLY BAPTISM, BOOK OF COMMON PRAYER

Healing, 1996

*I am the door;*
*if anyone enters by me,*
*he will be saved,*
*and will go in and out*
*and find pasture.*
—JOHN 10:9 RSV

Archway in Snow, 1996

*My Lord God, I have no idea where I am going. I do not see the road ahead of me. I cannot know for certain where it will end. Nor do I really know myself, and the fact that I think I am following your will does not mean that I am actually doing so. But I believe that the desire to please you does in fact please you. And I hope I have that desire in all that I am doing. I hope that I will never do anything apart from that desire. And I know that if I do this you will lead me by the right road, though I may know nothing about it. Therefore I will trust you always though I may seem to be lost and in the shadow of death. I will not fear, for you are ever with me, and you will never leave me to face my perils alone.*

—THOMAS MERTON

Let Me In, 1996

Katharine Gamble Scrantom was born into a social, fun-loving Episcopalian family in New Orleans, Louisiana, in 1958. She attended a girls' preparatory school, with a vigorous art program, and in her junior year fell in love with photography as a means of self-expression. Within the next year, as a seventeen-year-old high school senior, Katharine encountered Christ in a deep way. She knew, even then, art photography would become her vocation. She earned a Bachelor of Fine Arts degree in photographic design at the University of Georgia. In the last half of her senior year at the university, she met her future husband, Billy.

They married the next year, and lived in Columbus, Georgia, where Kathy opened her own studio, doing artistic and commercial photography. There, she exhibited in the Gardener Galleries, Art Uptown, and the Columbus Museum. Her black and white character study portraits led to a business in outdoor children's portraiture.

She moved to Sewanee, Tennessee with her husband, who studied in the School of Theology at the University of the South. While there, Kathy did some photographic portraiture, and began to photograph the life and pastorals of the university Domain. This book is Mrs. Scrantom's first published collection of photography as art.

She now resides in Albuquerque, New Mexico with her husband, her three children—Katie, Margaret, and Gamble, and their four-year old Sewanee dog, Lucky—whose life is a continual reminder to Kathy to follow God's path for her life.